DESTROYER AND PRESERVER

DESTROYER *AND* PRESERVER

MATTHEW ROHRER

WAVE BOOKS

Seattle & New York

Published by Wave Books

www.wavepoetry.com

Wave Books titles are distributed to the trade by

Consortium Book Sales and Distribution

Phone: 800-283-3572 / SAN 631-760X

This title is available in limited edition hardcover

directly from the publisher

Library of Congress Cataloging-in-Publication Data

Rohrer, Matthew.

Destroyer and preserver / Matthew Rohrer. — 1st ed.

p. cm.

ISBN 978-1-933517-50-6 (pbk.: alk. paper)

I. Title.

PS3568.O524D47 2011

811'.54—dc22

2010027092

Designed and composed by Quemadura

Printed in the United States of America

9 8 7 6 5 4 3 2 1

First Edition

Wave Books 026

for Seamus and Nola

DESTROYER AND PRESERVER

FROM MARS

We have some sad news
this morning
from Mars
the imagination thinks
in phrases but the universe
is a long sentence
according to our instruments
the oldest songs are
breaking apart
like a puzzle in a basement
every so often
we detect the smell
of marshmallows where
there are none the end
cannot be found
in the middle that's
a dream someone had
that our lives might
have meaning and not
just pop-up advertisements
but we have sad
news this morning
the dream has no
location or direction
and friends separated

by thousands of miles
are thinking of each
other simultaneously
but they have no idea
and we have no way
to reach them

WHAT IS MORE
DISTRACTING
THAN CLOUDS

Everything is more distracting than the clouds
they are never there they move on
no one can say remember that cloud
we saw in college it's still there
let's go see it again they walk their dogs in the park
they raise the plastic shade on the airplane window
and see a low region surrounded by thin peaks
all of it unreal white needle-shaped mountains like a scroll
of Chinese painting a landscape not even imagined
which disappears when the plane flies through it
and emerges in the blue air over the monotonous sorghum
    fields below
and everything changes a Diet Coke sprays open
the distracting flight attendant glides past
but the clouds continue to gather
they fail and dissipate they come from the east
where the sea makes them foam
or they come from the west
full of ragweed and pollen too small to see
everyone breathes it all day
distracted by a song a friend sings

over and over white miraculous shifts overhead
the clouds reflected in the surface of a cocktail
completely ignored drink and cloud ignored
while a woman takes her clothes off in front of a man
who smiles shaded by the passing helicopter's rotors
tearing up the stratus clouds and flinging now
her shirt at him
rain falling in her almost unnaturally light blue eyes
when he looks closely reflected there
in the morning the whole sky
is a lusty pink lamp turned on
a little girl stands openmouthed in her pajamas
she is his daughter it is five o'clock in the morning
the city still sleeps the clouds fly out to sea
how many people saw them this morning
the citizens who turn their backs on the leaves and insects
who turn their faces to the light of their rooms
when the clouds are the color and shape of flaming brigantines
gone up in a dark harbor but they're distracted
from the mare's tails if they looked up they'd see
there's nothing to be afraid of
a high-pressure system is moving in the air is cooler now
the sky is a mild blue something
has changed

POETS WITH HISTORY/
POETS WITHOUT HISTORY

I have a secret I will now reveal

I believe it is possible to tell if someone is interesting

or not simply by looking into his eyes

on the train each morning it is hard for me

not to stare at each person variously sleeping

or listening to music, to see who she really is

but this is difficult to pull off

among the guarded patriots, the fearful,

everyone talks all day on their little phones

to their mothers, *mama*, they say,

mama, I had a bad dream

when they haven't slept,

in the rumble of big cars moving slowly

on the city streets a ghost removes his heart

and falls through the clouds

and the melting icebergs crumple

like a prisoner shot in the side

I move through the days remarkably sinuously

and spinning inside

I wash the dishes two or three times a day

with the hot water on and on

like a dream behind the yellow gloves

from which I too cannot awaken

though my son is done with school

and holds my hand on the walk home

the feeling of falling backwards

into the bed at night fills me

each time

with sweet content

all the people rounded up in camps

have a look in their eyes

that can't reach us now

GHOST

A ghost floats over the courtyard
only three windows with lights

in the kitchen with my face on the glass
when everyone in the house is asleep

and I see the ghost light of the cloudy houses
under the stars
and the ghost light of all the laundry

the look of the house
in the dark is clean

only the essential things
can find their tongues and speak

as I glide without edges
through the rooms
like the smell of cooking
I do not belong to anything but books
which is very sad

I want to kiss someone

the whole world is asleep

MARQUE NÚMERO DOS

But then the day got
away from me
holding the phone
to my left ear for 45
minutes para español
marque número dos
for someone else's appointment
was lost or I fell
into a hole and no one
could see me
pulling on my face
or hear me screaming
and then I just hung up
and walked out into the blue bloom
of love and needed to eat
I ignored the phone
at what peril? the rooms
swelled a bit to fit my new silence
and my shirts were on
the floor. There was no one
could touch me
a sunny day
is a sufficient cathedral
though I have not finished with you
Doctor Wong

DULL AFFAIRS

How am I to concentrate
on the heavy and dull
affairs of state
with the sound of a baby having a dream
in the other room
the individual should not turn
away though the cup is rattled
in his face or the dogwood
is bent into the path
that is for the state to ignore
it cannot change
it is like the sound of a baby crying out
that is only imagined
it is much worse
a small cloud
that looks like an enormous flea
crouches over the city
but no one looks up
they pound the ground
when they need water
they dig a well
what is the state to them
they are not heavily
invested in darkness

THEY PULL A SUICIDE
FROM THE WATER

I put the girl to sleep
in a drawer on the floor
in the couple-colored air
the windows are enormous
the blogs are good
the blogs are bad
and there is a vibrato
in the courtyard
when a woman sings
the gendarmes park on the corner
and no one is afraid
they walk beside the river
in the dark
they pull a suicide from the water
I clip my toenails out the window
it is going to rain

THE SMELL OF
FRYING FISH

The smell of frying fish
drove me to the fire escape
the sun took its time
filling the harbor
with ashes
sandpipers moved
they were controlled
by song
I saw my neighbor
the pencil
turn sideways
in front of her mirror
she stepped into her wineglass
as the sun brought everything
a little closer to raspberries

POEM FOR MUSIC'S
DISTRACTIONS

I wasn't paying attention and ate all the leftover pork tenderloin
Through a crashing surf of sleep the baby is drenched
And in my dreams I got down to the work I'd put off
N. looked at me oddly it really shook me
I returned to my chamber and locked the door and trembled
In the morning the cold air around the window welcomes me back
Erik Satie as performed on guitar sparkles against the glass
My wife says "I hate the winter" lying on the carpet
All around me demons clasp their hands behind their backs and smile
That was hours ago I'm still full "maybe I'll make some popcorn"
I'm lightning-swift I leap into bed I wrap the sheets around my neck
In the stars a great tortoise hangs its head and begins to sing

POEM FOR STARLINGS

When you try to make a joke
in a bank
it falls flat
there's an armed guard
standing there
wearing sunglasses indoors
motionless
but no one laughs
in fact my intentions
are misunderstood
no, no, I am just
going to walk out
the door and come back in
to turn my coins
into paper money
$53
in the sunshine
I'm on my way
with my jacket
in my backpack
and the steel
grates over the pubs
early afternoon
my step as high
as the starlings

bickering in the sky
the birdsong
of the city
and the paper lifting off
the sidewalks
goodbye, I wish
the world were different

BELIEVE

In the morning humidity
on the windows he
throws up and cries
out strange it took

so long to feel
bad he slept all
night I have to
go to work I

have to cut the
right wire or everything
blows up but first
I will read Apollinaire

In the room they
all take books seriously
talking about them the
sun sets over the

park while they do
the little lights come
on I can see
them from the subway

I'm reading *The Sleepers* on
the way to Brooklyn
a spooky girl passes
in another train

One time late at
night on the F
train a girl asked
me what I was

reading it was a
biography of Coleridge she
abruptly sat back down
what is my true

fate it's a good
life the magnolia scrapes
the window my love
is crossing the river

I was on a
blanket in the park
with my daughter I
saw a plane make

a turn you don't
usually see I notice
everything and have lived
here a long time

black unmarked vehicles appeared
in front of the
bagel place a part
of me wants oblivion

A woman with too
many teeth is a
mother at my son's
school I back away

the sun is terribly
bright on her she
smiles at me I
look down at the

sidewalk I'm a little
hungover that night they
rise from their table
and steal my car

Motherfucker stole my car
and that was my
grandma's car I liked
how it looked here

in the city with
some stickers on it
the police just nodded
it had my grandfather's

three-pound hammer in
the trunk there is
no place on the
form to put this

The joke newspaper said
and I mean the
one that admits it
is a joke that

hundreds of millions of
people you will never
talk to disagree with
you like a bell

my face started to
twitch I pushed my
daughter through a city
I still believed in

How come the body
rejects the medicine when
it is good no
one knows no one

has ever come back
to tell us if
it hurts everyone is
worried they'll raise taxes

I thought of a
gentler way to rid
us of the ants
we could just wait

CASUALTIES

My son says
are soldiers good or bad?
I say it's very complicated.

He brushes his teeth
with a toothbrush
that looks like a whale.

I see his face, his eyes
right in front of mine.
We are drowning together

in the hold of a ship.
He looks just like me.
The rain slows outside.

One cloud turns pink at sunset.
A bomb falls on a house in the desert.
The plane that dropped it

glides through another blue
and returns to us
to be washed and put away.

MY VOTE

I lift my voice
in song passed out
breathless halfway up
a staircase. I lift my voice
in song in the small bed—
linen hangs and glows
in outside influence.
Winter gets into everything,
the small of her back
broken off
in the night.
Winter moves
her fingers to the sea,
her promontories are locked
in ice
and I am just one man
my vote doesn't actually count

TWO HOURS OF CRYING

Two hours of crying in his crib, then sleep.
Snow again & dreams of her
beat against the windows in this
sharpened air: come home & be my blanket.
He sleeps on. Things around the apartment,
some of them, start to shimmer. Everyone
in their cars, driving at top speed outside.
He's still asleep, it's only been seven
minutes. I must keep myself awake or
be visited with horrors. My love
hurtling toward me through vast subway
tunnels in one hour & twenty minutes.
I am a dream a black obelisk dreams
& forgets. I haven't
put much thought into it. I just feel good.

RODINA

Rodina I thought that was your name
and I was wrong
but I'm going to keep thinking it
it's too late to look back
you are a black angel
not of death but of
the darkness in the spring
lying back on the stone beneath you
in the cemetery
deer come to pursue you
but you never move
a black heavy exhaustion upon you
thank you for your blessing
of love, it flowered
it spread into the sun
when I close my eyes
it really is you
swept up in the distant
thunder creeping up to surround
the house

FOR WHICH I LOVE YOU

For a while it seemed like
we wouldn't the window
was open January night
but then you
and so I
and then we
quite slowly
as new rockets arc
through the desert blue
skies you said who
could actually take pleasure
in that kind of hate
for which I love you
and cover you
with kisses
the night doesn't have
a clear shot if I wrap
you up and then sleep
comes like a dark flood
rising up around the bed
our only fear will the baby awake?
and dreams that complicate
things their velocity
is a mystery but if we
stay there you don't
have to leave in the morning

AT THE DEUX MAGOTS

No one cares what the song
is they spear filets
of tiny fish from their bowls
and laugh at the ceiling
how lonely this is, the night
has already fallen on the hills
and the vineyards where
the night is bottled but
the light won't go out
the family of man gathers
at the river to drink in
the dusk and accordions
kicking up the dust, the girls
pop champagne into the trees
and the heaviness parts
the waves—oh this is why
the Romans gave up
and died—the lamp
of hope burns even
though I cannot move
my arms and legs, the sun
is gone but not the day
I read a little book of Shelley
I wonder where he stayed
if I read *Stanzas Written*
in Dejection one more time

the leaves on the trees
are sure to separate from me
each moment seems totally real
until I fall into the bed
and dream
torches light the way for me

INSIDE OUT

I rose with the sun
through a shower of raindrops
timed perfectly and
hugged his plane around the neck I
meant to use both arms
which was true I really
missed him and he came
from L.A. to tell me
to turn left just beyond a
wet bird on a building like
our topic of conversation
who remains a mystery
his first book was just fine
we gave him an A minus and my eyes
glazed and drifted into feeling bad
but I laughed
when he said
the law endures
like lines of icing
in the traffic
the rain
removes the people's
sense of community
they have to keep moving
there is a sphere

that touches everyone
the Honda Civic is responsive
to life and music
between the two rivers
where my grandfather served
the church in a war
that will never end
clearing snow from the streets
putting down uprisings with nickels
I think the future
belongs to the ghosts
sweeping the sidewalks
with their wedding dresses

POEM WITH THE
TITLE AT THE END

I think my son will be OK
he said duh everyone looks different
when they explained who
Martin Luther King Jr. was
I think the mayor was terrified
into speaking the truth
on the radio that the real
heroes of the war are
the people
they rushed him
into a safe room
as he toured the region
a rocket was coming
like a crow in a storm
because violence can't stop
violence she said
and I agreed it makes
perfect sense if they hate
you and you kill their
families where can you go
the appropriate response
is to inhabit your dreams
only to emerge for a sandwich

and if the appropriate response
is a fist to the throat
that is a serious business
you retreat into the self completely
where the dream has no
landscape just a color
an emotion a conversation
that pulls the birds from
the sky and they lie
in a feathered heap
like Rumi at the end
of the night when the hill
turned blue behind him
and now lies quiet
beneath a jug of wine
this poem has been called
YOUR POLITICS ARE DUST

SKYWARD

We have some sad news
this morning from Mars
I heard tiny feet approaching over
the roof my wife was
still asleep the poison still

paralyzed me it might be
noon before I could parent
correctly sad beeps rained down
from transmitters long dead when
the blue jay debuted his composition

in the magnolia the mournful
sounds of the garbagemen approaching
then moving on contain a message
put it in a can
and launch it skyward

THE TERRORISTS

1

A terrorist walks into a bar
he gets a beer
nothing has ever tasted better
and nothing draws him
through the air afterwards
into a cloud of grackles
by the harbor
the whole thing started
because of beauty
his love of beauty
it was all a big joke beauty
played on love
a ferry chugs
to the residential island
or the setting sun
the bright belly
of a helicopter
pauses overhead
removing birds
another ferry comes out
of the sun
and crashes gently
into the old tires

at the dock
he decides again to stop
drinking for a week
a song enters his head
at this point
to drive out thought
a long time later he has
to pee and walks back
to the bar
pausing
barely perceptible
though internally vast
with birdsong

2

A bright green bird alighted
on the handlebars
of her bike
while she stared
at the rooftop
white heat haze
and no signal
not even the dust stirred
and when she finally looked
down at the bird
it changed to a leaf

He walked his son
to school every morning
and returned for him
in the afternoon.
Besides that he was
very patient. He waited
for a phone call. He imagined
what it would be like
to pick up that phone call.
Whenever the phone rang
he imagined he was about to
pick up the long-awaited call
what would it feel like?
what would he see
out his window
as he answered the phone?
or would the call's importance
cloud his sight?
Many times his phone rang
but it was not the phone call.
His son left home
and the neighborhood changed
no one's children returned
with their children
a stone porch across the street collapsed
one early morning
with a small, explosive
sound.

4

The longest week
of the year
continual sunlight
a police helicopter circling
the traffic circle
while she pushes
her daughter on the swing
the accusation of the fountains
murmurs *do it*
and her daughter
turns into the rhythm
of her arms
she will do it
she will do it soon
the other parents
are like enormous empty
cakes shining in the park
and she hasn't eaten in two days
warm breeze
lifting the hairs
on her arms

5

She was on the bus
but this was not
the time

this was just going
to the grocery store
she was just sitting
facing forwards
this was not about
the ruling class
she could feel her child's leg
against hers when the bus
accelerated
this was not about anything
to her, she stared straight ahead
down the street into the bright haze
a little girl
misbehaved in the seat next to her
but her eyes were unfocused
she was scattered
into the distance
a great heaviness kept her
from drawing herself back in
to see, she only heard the child
the fake hysterical raging could not
really find her
the next stop was the grocery store
she was tired of regular apples
she was going to get a Fuji apple

DISPLAY CASE OF STEAK

The pill stands between me
and the display case of steak

a song gets inside
and becomes a thought

the gesture of rubbing the hands
over the face to indicate

a thumb that doesn't work
a little emotional pain

that's the rhythm of being attentive
to the wine in your arteries

they say, and I say,
whose dream is this anyway?

before wetting the bed. The verse
is projected across the room

hits the wall, slides to
the baseboards. One of the cats

examines it and moves along.
Everyone knows there is more to life

than this lying supine
on the cheap rug in the middle

of a family

DRINKING WITH
YOUR BROTHER

Drinking with your brother
on the boardwalk
a foggy Thursday night

fifty people
in medieval
burgundy robes

walk by quietly
the police
have caught a sand shark

you're at home
I think sitting
still with a light

in you glowing
in the living room
I almost hear

country music
and smell your breath
the atomized ginger

still in your hair
from this morning
I have wanted to say

for eighteen years
something like the muezzin
says from the tower

about you
that all people will believe
and they will turn

off their televisions then
and lie down on their beds
in the dark looking

out into the night
where a storm
pulls itself up

out of a sea fog
to be noticed
and they notice

the storm in other things
the plovers shooting out
of the night

into the surf
their voices
faintly white

POEM FOR MIDEAST PEACE

The temple rocks a little back and forth
All the same notes rise out of the different strings
Or behold a cup of wine that hasn't spilled in 4,000 years
It's all the same to me in the winter I'll take a nap
If the baby takes a nap too it is cosmic
I just leaned my head back on the couch and felt like I was falling
Like a stuffed toy they drop to the refugees, a poisoned toy
All the suits that are pressed to have this meeting are in a pile
A song that blends perfectly with the drowsy trees
By the water's edge it sweeps away our footprints
When one person yearns for another you can hear it in the sunset
Then an explosion tears the hair off a bus driver
The desert is glad to accept this blood it is our mistake
You should never look back

POEM FOR MY THIRTIES

We interrupt this poem to read The Itsy Bitsy Spider five times
    in a row
Indiana so nice we went there twice
Then an ancestral vision on a silent night, snow beating the little
    building
They came to stand around me neither happy nor sad
Miss Mary Mack three times on the floor
Sunny & dry autumn day, the truck spun out on cinders
We fishtailed and flopped on our side & stopped, we could hear
    the sunlight
I sledded through my very worst hangover
All this meditating on how close- or wide-set are the eyes
Or the straight drop of snow from the fjord into the bay
Poignant & persistent absence of the elves
It's all the same to me who Caesar drapes with laurel leaves
I have a tin of them in the kitchen I use for making soup

ENOUGH WITH ABSTRACTION

1

You have to have
a fly's eyes to
see this a form
has someone attached to it
it is like
going to church for
the very young
the mystery seems within reach
and someone's hand did
this we think we
see an ancient alphabet
of paint on canvas
within reach or a mind
enough with abstraction
we all said we
never agreed
with emotional corruption
that girl walking
into the next gallery
what about her ass

Doctor why do I feel
like this a mysterious
overcast daydream lives in
my bedroom which I
cannot escape by bus
or book I think
I like my own
mind when I see
this the real title
of this poem is
"an early work by
Philip Guston" or the
love of two sisters
which is impossible to
attain that is the
art of the bedroom
a little disorder   roses

WHERE THE HAWK PAUSES

I have a heart
it is too big for my clothes
a word pulls it from its sleep

some nights the city
cannot contain it

the bright blue
continuously fills with you

and your hair is in the bathtub

where the hawk pauses
near the playground
to clean the blood off
my heart goes to him

every morning you travel
the length and breadth of my heart
and nowhere are you free
often your train is delayed

NEW MEXICO

New Mexico stares into the clouds.
The air is as empty as a dream,
no heaviness, no regret.
Dune hawks and grosbeaks
return to the holes in the cliffs
where people lived. They lived and thrived
and dyed their clothes in tannin from the creek.
The stars came down at night much closer
than the jimsonweed. And they spoke
and they said what we say.
And the boils suppurated on their arms.
A thin pathway of charcoal smoke
directed them to the sky.
At night the rivers of stars astonish me—
I go get my sister, the sky is the beginning,
we are the tourists. Voices call out
from the hard pines—a pale power
moves through the branches.

A SUNNY LUNCH

Waiting under the umbrella
for the baby to fall asleep

and then to the battlements!
I haven't seen you

in a long time
a more adamantine twinkle

in your eye
let's take a walk when this is over

it will never be over
we'll all have to walk together

into a sunny lunch
of crisp cod cakes

on lettuce, not enough,
and too much Riesling

I think now about sleep
as a poem's greatest gift

while I fool with it
in my head in the dark

and you drive down Alvarado
by the taqueria and are struck

by an enormous car
and evacuated to a church

into its big black hands
and petted to sleep

and forget your car
and the lives of the later caesars

your letters to Felice
were intercepted

I have to tell you this
because the police

are on every corner
and none of us is safe

FLOWERS

The most spectacular address
in American expatriotism
remains in the shade
until just after 1300 hours
I go boil my head
in my bedroom
until every bell begins
to clang for freedom
even the tiniest chimes
on the belly dancers
the light green cones
of the cedars too
that want out of the house
where the open window
like a ghost in daylight
blows its kisses and falls asleep
and remains there
content to be a small part
of history
while I urge
my chariot to the hippodrome

POEM ON THE OCCASION OF
THE MIDTERM ELECTION

Dream Brazil is a wash—
too expensive. Dream Antarctica again
and the cold feels good.
And I look all right there
in the big blue coat.
I never wanted to impress
anybody, so I kept it
unremarkable. The plain truth is
not enough now to change
the empire into a flower.
It is already a hummingbird
in an endless loop. *No
no*, they say, there's power
still in children and old
people. There's power in swarming
the neighbors and refusing to
die. There's power in songs.
It's we who are powerless.

PIE

Throwing shit we don't need away
vacuuming up cat hair
that's what I did today
I imagined it was morning
all day, beautiful weather
that didn't follow me inside
stillness in afternoon
rooms, a Hammond organ
shadows of leaves
on white curtains
in the past, lost
in the beautiful crashing surf
an imperfect gift
I feel it if I think
about Li Po
drinking wine until
the pleasant sinking
of the ego into the night
and then he drank a lot
more and became sozzled
and drowned off
a little boat.
"Called back."
And he never tasted pie.

DIPTYCH

A chair by Thonet
which does not make
your ass look big
like futurism does
it is an outworn creed
it never stood up
and did anything about the war
from where you are sitting
it remains perfectly still
I will bring you a drink
in the idea of a glass

*

I've been studying minutiae
for the past twenty years—in the public
baths—of the American inferno—and
I've been translating from the language
of the crickets—beneath the streetlights
in Paris—in utter blue surprise—and I have
been haunted—by the cold hands
of the polar bears—where the thin withy
bush grows—like the map of the subway—
the green heads of the dead in piles—beneath
the stars—with the star men treading lightly—

I wore a suit to the races—and pulled
the trigger—when they asked me—
I called the red foot down—
on the lawful gathering—for which I won
a medal—burning a hole through
the clouds—there was very little blood—just ash—

POEM FOR ASTHMA

Hold on while I do a breathing exercise
I am just paying attention to myself, or the universe is vast
And the universe is imperfect, I stop what I'm doing and look
    right at it
I say "Doc is this thing going to kill me?"
He pronounces it "asmer"; a voice calls me from a tower before
    sunrise
Or in a terrible panic I bite through my own mouth & am pinned
    to the floor
I am clubbed in the head by a wintry cloud
Am pulled bodily from my dream
 "Oh, absolutely man" is my answer to everything

POEM FOR THE WIND

There's a ghost that moves against the land
It's all the same to me if the wires are down, I'm not going anywhere
We stayed sitting up in bed while you ripped the paint off our car
The damage you do to my mind all night, you blow on its embers,
    it won't go out
You come like a lover to us these summer evenings
And walk away to have a drink, to shout about it
Nagoya forest is as far as we make it, beside the sparkling harbor
You rattle all night & I dream of losing power in a tiny plane
Or I pedaled & did not move & the storm moved into me
A chill and then nothing, I felt like a dog
Once I drank you from our Oldsmobile all summer
You push a crate of eggs downhill and we laugh, we do nothing
Today you come from every direction at once

MARY WOLLSTONECRAFT
TRAVELING WITH HER KIDS

Mary Wollstonecraft
traveling with her kids.
She was very brave.
They rolled over the earth
underneath the sun
only rarely drawing attention to themselves.
Or they floated like a cork in a great bay
of cognac. That is why
I haven't called.

The sun is furiously at it again
when you are still asleep.
In my mind it is all green
and gold where we were,
like a light through a mug of beer.
Or I am driving you to Queens
sick at heart and high
in the backseat
in the sere heat off the BQE.
A window has been left open.
The poppies give you confidence
and they take it away, that is all
I have to say about them,

I can't be their friend anymore.
2:32 p.m. My mouth is watering.
A darkness on my heart
despite the weather,
nothing between
my hat and the planets.
I walked through the park
to the library writhing
like a terrible serpent.
I felt like Shelley. To love
the world and hate its face.
Then Planned Parenthood called.
I gave them $50 more.
This calmed me down.
To stay out of the fight,
but to egg it on.

POEM FOR GERMAN HERITAGE

I smell vinegar and cabbage my heart is braised meat
In my gothic script I post these notices on your doors
A fine rain that falls but can't touch me in the forest
Or I come out of the trees with my father & our guide to stand at
    a precipice
He asks us if we feel all their eyes on us, the little men of the trees
Deep roots like the soul of a mountain cry out "I'm trapped!"
"I can't breathe!"
When you come upon me in the night, there'll be nothing, just the
    smell of edelweiss
Would you march against me with your army of giants?
For I have an army of midgets, we belong together
In your chamber or the parade ground I have cut them all loose
The women I am drawn to live across the mountains

NOT QUESTIONS

I have to give in
to a dark energy
eating constantly
and falling asleep
on the couch
under a wool blanket
red, black, and yellow
and a color made
when red meets black
today feels like fall
my thumb hurts
from never learning to write
I hold the pen wrong
like the fat man
who limps slowly
from his basement
to the main road
the Burger King
and slowly back
three times a day
too young, too young
some drug put him
in its back pocket
and forgot

my grandparents watch
this from their porch
what is his name?
they've lived there
since 1960 making
no improvements
sitting on the davenport
never giving in
to the dark energy
but going to church
while the town unravels
around them and now
the prison will be shut
down—will the prisoners
be let go?
Don't answer that.
I had hoped to have
something to tell you
and not questions
after I stuck my hand
right into the wall
and pulled it out
wall and arm unscathed
feeling around blindly
in the stream of dark
energy, actually walking differently
now—in the dark, walking
not to awaken
the oak

in the forest
to pass lightly, no louder
than the modulation
of the creek in its bed
and pass out of town
unheard and unheard-from
even if it breaks their hearts

GOODMORNING

When you stand in front of the mirror
admiring your belly and I am still
in bed, your smooth calves, the humid
air that wakes up the city,

there is a look in your eyes
I would blindly fly a plane into.
Goodmorning. My head is ringing
and the furniture is still stoned.

Like a demobilized Germany you are secretly
building up an arsenal in you but unlike
Germany you are filled with love.
The governance of fear will be checked with love.

RED FLOWERS

I don't know what
kinds of flowers they'll be
until they open
and then they do
and I don't know
my son bought them
for my wife they open
in a gray beer stein on the table
they're dying or they
are technically
already dead but
to us who live each moment
over and over again
they open beautifully
for a few days
like a houseguest
and when the sun
through the white
Roman curtains
lit up her newborn face
it was terribly
small with a
foreboding that filled

the afternoon—
I see you, I see you,
I whispered to her
but I would never see her like
this again

WU WEI

Why isn't it easy

to sit still, I said

spreading bleu cheese

on a date, it's easy

to sit here

but everyone wants everything

to be perfect and cry

when they can't make it happen

I said, and he said

he forgot what he was going

to say but it was going

to be something about

compassion falling back

on the earth in a white

rain of petals, and she said

wu what? Like water

I said, yielding

to the rock but wearing it down,

like you, he said,

meaning me, and she said

like how? Like given

the choice to do something

stupid or to sit in a chair

everyone leaps up

with their eyes ablaze

he said, when the greatest

art is to turn back

which she thought about

while I considered a little pickle

their desire is killing them

he said, and everyone else,

she added, which is why

we turn back from the sky,

he said, to them

with our hands to gently

lay them on their foreheads,

which sometimes works

I said, if dreams work

ACKNOWLEDGMENTS

Some poems in *Destroyer and Preserver* first appeared in the following journals: *Alhambra Poetry Calendar 2010, Brooklyn Rail, Calaveras, The Iowa Review, La Petite Zine, Maggy, The Morning News, Painted Bride Quarterly, Paperbag, Pulchritudinous Review, Salt Hill, Smartish Pace,* and *Splash of Red.* Grateful thanks to all of the editors and volunteers who make these and all the little magazines possible.